# Effective Continuous Improvement

*Harnessing the Kaizen approach to create a system for effective change*

**Disclaimer**:

The author of this book has tried to present the most accurate information to his knowledge at the time of writing. This book is intended for information purposes only. The author does not imply any results to those using this book, nor are they responsible for any results brought about by the usage of the information contained herein.

# Table of Contents

# Introduction

Welcome.

Thank you for downloading this book, I hope it helps you to design your own continuous improvement system or to rejuvenate your current approach.

I decided to write this book as a way to stimulate interest in continuous improvement, particularly for those of you who have tried it but failed to get the results you wanted.

As I will discuss, continuous improvement can be a low cost way to both engage more actively with your workforce and create improvements that actually benefit your profit, customers and your team.

The book is broken down into several sections. After the introductory pages, which include some relevant examples, I will take you through a number of approaches and tools you can use to generate improvement ideas. After this we will look at how to take your continuous improvement ideas and turn them into a system you can use to manage, monitor to ensure progress.

The first method, focal points, was the original stimulus for me writing this book. A number of my consulting clients were struggling to maintain a flow of projects for their improvement activities. After realising what their problem was I developed the method I will describe and found it was incredibly well received. The tool was then used with subsequent clients who had similar problems and it yielded the same benefit – a torrent of improvement ideas.

This is the second edition of this book. The first version focused primarily on the focal points method but I realised that my readers were looking for a few options to consider before they started to design their way of working. For that reason this version has been expanded accordingly.
As I said at the start, I hope you find this short book helpful in your quest to develop and manage your own continuous improvement activities.

All the best,

Giles

# Why Do Continuous Improvement?

It seems that the term 'continuous improvement' keeps going round and round. Is this because it is so good, or because most organisations have not learned how to master it? The answer is probably both, but there are a lot of businesses that perform continuous improvement in fits and starts, so 'occasional improvement' is probably a more fitting title for them.

The name 'continuous improvement' should be a clue to the approach you are intending to take. It shouldn't stop and this book offers a handful of simple methods you can use to keep the momentum going. I believe that some of the main reasons that businesses don't continuously improve is due to two main factors. The first factor is the visibility of improvements. By this I mean that many businesses need to fix parts of their business that obviously aren't working. This is good, but moving your business from bad to OK is only part of the journey. Improvements shouldn't stop just because things are OK. Creating methods to help your business move from OK to brilliant is the reason that this book was written. Pace is the other factor hindering continuous improvement; people can feel burned out if the process of improvement isn't managed effectively. If there isn't a process then you can often find your business is trying to improve everything at once. Not only does this become difficult to manage from a logistics / time perspective, but the burden of undergoing change can take its toll. Regulating the pace of change is as important as the identification and planning for the change.

And what about the things you have already improved? Well, things only stay the same for a while. Once you have lived with the improvement for a while, not only do you know more about the function or activity you have improved, but you also have customers who are prepared for even better service. So, why not be better? This is the essence of continuous improvement and the ideas in this book will help you engage with this approach more effectively.

There are many good reasons to undertake continuous improvement including, having happier customers and happier staff, beating off the competition, winning new work and increasing your profits.

It is likely that you experience pressures from customers and competition so you have a direct need to improve - it doesn't need to be difficult and this book can help you implement a way of improving that can impress your customers. Your clients deserve the best service possible, so why not make sure it is you who gives the best service and not the competition?

You can get your staff engaged with the business through continuous improvement. Why not get more out of you staff by using their brains?

When you improve how your business works then you have the potential to make more profit. Coming up with better ways of working can decrease your costs, increase your capacity and help to win new work.

As chaos and day-to-day hassles reduce through continuous improvement you can make life easier for yourself and your staff. Leaving work on time, leaving work at work and building harmony between teams are all good reasons to practice continuous improvement. In one month's time you will still be at work doing the same tasks so you might as well do them better.

Many businesses 'blitz' the workplace and this can be useful but these periodic improvements can't be your only strategy; continuous improvement needs to be ongoing.

You can make continuous improvement a simple process, easy to get involved with and repeatable. So why not take advantage of the benefits mentioned above if it can be done in a painless, effective and engaging way?

# What This Book Intends to Do

The field of Lean Manufacturing / Lean Services is so big nowadays that I need to make it crystal clear what this book is aiming to help you do.

Firstly, the book aims to share with you a number of improvement approaches. Some will resonate with you more than others. All will help you to generate ideas, but you need to find which ones work best with your team and your style. There are five methods shared in this book. I hope that you find one that fits you and your business.

Secondly, the book covers ideas on capturing and managing the ideas. The purpose of this is to help you take your business past one off improvements and into continuous improvement.

This book does not have all of the answers, but has been written with the intention of helping you to find some methods that you can trial and make your own in your pursuit of developing and running an excellent business.

# Common Problems with Continuous Improvement

There are many valid reasons why businesses don't keep up (or even implement) continuous improvement approaches. This section lists some of those issues so that you can be aware of them as you progress through your own experience.

When businesses become really busy they sometimes go into a feral state. If you think of the term feral (wild, animal like) children, these businesses go back into a basic state of operation. For many people that means running around, working harder and longer. At the same time we often hear phrases such as 'we don't have time to operate the correct process'. Instead of running around even more, this is the ideal time to stop, think and act on what needs to happen. Working harder usually doesn't solve these types of problems - especially when the business is struggling from the resultant poor performance.

Returning to a feral state often results in processes degrading. If there is no immediate penalty for changing the process (from cutting out steps) then the risk is that the process changes permanently. It could be that the process does not need the disregarded steps, but it may be that that it does. I add this point purely to raise your awareness of the issue. I see many businesses that go through a busy period, drop something that appears superfluous only to later find that it is really important. Consequential thinking can go out the window; improving a process to adapt to changing volumes when the time comes can be a really good strategy, rather than simply hoping for the best!

Furthermore, there is often the issue that it's hard to stop and improve; many people are so busy that they will not stop to work out a better way to do what they are currently struggling with.

This is made even more difficult because in many cases you don't know what or how to improve. The term continuous improvement can seem vague and apply to anything. However, it is possible to create an approach to direct your focus so that you can make this particular issue go away. That is the purpose of this book, to guide and direct your efforts into the specific areas that you can improve.

Another problem is that businesses often focus on the wrong things to improve. This can often be based on knee jerk reactions rather than smooth controlled progression from an improvement perspective. Using the frameworks proposed in this book can reduce this issue greatly. Having a systematic approach can help communicate the method and can make it easier to control and to follow.

Finally, another issue is that time seems to run away from us and so we don't get around to making improvements. There are ways around this and we will explore them in this book too.

# Analogy

When you boil continuous improvement down to its basic parts it is quite a simple process. When you add in the pressures of day-to-day working then you can understand why many businesses don't action their ideas, or even remember how to continuously improve.

A really good analogy is when babies are learning to walk. If you have ever watched a small child doing this they will keep going until they have mastered walking, they don't stop after a prescribed number of attempts. They experiment with lots of different ways of walking (grabbing objects, staggering, crawling variations etc...) rather than (necessarily) sticking to a defined plan. And, they are both focussed and determined.

I should stress here that crawling is OK. Babies don't need to walk, do they? They can now move around, arguably their job is done. This is analogous to the comment I made earlier about moving from bad to OK. In this case 'bad' is no mobility and 'OK' is some mobility. Consider your own business; have you and your team improved something so that the immediate (visible) problems have gone away but have not then gone on to fully explore just how good it can be?

If little kids can iterate how they perform then we as adults can do exactly the same in our businesses.

If we look more closely at the above analogy we may consider these ideas:

- Continuous improvement involves trial and error, but with a clear focus on what we need to achieve.
- There needs to be a purpose to our activity.
- We can't just stop after one go, we need to keep going until we achieve / surpass the desired result.

So, if little kids can do it then there is no reason why we can't as well.

# Examples

The following examples are here to give some context to this book. If you are struggling with your own continuous improvement approach, or haven't started yet, then these examples will hopefully give you some food for thought. This book will show you how to put these ideas, and more, into practise.

## Example One - Manufacturer Gets Lost Amongst the Ideas

A manufacturer had decided to create a channel for improvement ideas. The concept was pushed forward because it sounded good and they believed that everyone else was doing the same thing (or more importantly - their competitors).

When the doors were opened to receive improvement ideas there was a surge of suggestions, most of which were supplied without all of the necessary facts and information. The person running the programme found that they spent most of their time trying to fathom out what these ideas really were.

Occasionally there was a good idea in the pile and it made the overall efforts of running the programme worthwhile - for the first three months. After this time the influx dried up and the people who had submitted less usable suggestions felt ignored because there was no formal way of logging the ideas and feeding back to the individuals what was happening with their ideas.

After the 'scheme' had fizzled out I got involved and reviewed the successes and failures to date. A system was then introduced so that the people who contributed to the suggestions were still part of the loop even if they were not seeing their ideas implemented.

To support the system we created a rota of activity that cycled continuously, providing focus and guidance as to what we were going to improve in the business and how we were going to improve it. As we also now had a system to manage the improvement suggestions we could also take on board the 'random' suggestions that were appearing.

Through better control of the improvement focus, prioritisation of the ideas and better communication across the business, results started to stream through like clockwork.

This approach was simple, consistent and focussed.

## Example Two - Retailer Can't Get Started with Continuous Improvement

A small business that bought and sold products knew that they needed to improve how they were conducting business; they just didn't know where to start. There were some obvious areas of improvement that needed to happen immediately when I got involved. From this point of view there were two phases that needed to happen. The first was to clean up some of the issues that were happening to stop the vast majority of the fire fighting that was taking place. The second phase was to calmly move forwards with the rest of the business from an improvement perspective.

Before I got involved there had been some attempts at improving, but there had been a lack of focus and hence no real results to speak of. This meant that they just needed a change of approach to get them moving.

Together we created a framework to give focus to their improvements. By breaking down the job of continuously improving their business into small manageable packets we were able to leave them with a sustainable method for making improvements.

With small steps being taken by the staff they soon started to gain some momentum with their changes.

The real result here, however, was that as they started to get better and better, their customers noticed. Over time word of mouth helped them to sell even more products because they had made a name for themselves as being a slick and reliable supplier.

## Example Three – He Had the Ideas All Along!

This example takes me back to my days as a Production Manager. I had seven Team Leaders report to me when I ran a factory's operations and some were more engaged than others. The Team Leader I had the least engagement with however was the one who ran the two departments that were struggling the most.

My attempts to force progress were futile, all my ideas were rejected and performance was stuck in low gear. My persistence paid off however when I backed off a little bit and didn't try to force the issues so much. Eventually myself and this Team Leader came to an understanding and he became willing to try some of the ideas that we had discussed.

The first idea had some merits and we saw some marginal gains in performance. We tried the second idea and the same thing happened, as it did for the third.

The really interesting bit in this example came when the Team Leader came to me, without prompting, to ask if he could test out one of his ideas. After checking the Health and Safety implications of what he suggested he and his team conducted a trial. It was a rip roaring success and effectively doubled the capacity of his department (something that we had been struggling with). The improvement cost us forty five minutes of his team's time and utilised unwanted or unused items of kit to modify an oven. I was staggered by the result.

This wasn't the end either. This Team Leader then went on to improve many other facets of his department and transformed the quality and performance of how the department operated.

It was an amazing transformation to witness and the business certainly noticed the improvements in performance (which he was duly recognised for).

The point of this example is that the people around you usually have lots and lots of good ideas trapped within their minds. It is your job as a leader to help bring out these ideas. Many times it is just a case of taking away the obstacles to let the ideas come forth.

The ideas in this book will hopefully allow you to develop your own continuous improvement approach so that you can also achieve similar, or better, results than those described above.

# Getting Your Team Ready

Before you read about the continuous improvement methods that I am going to put forward in this book I would like you to think about your general approach toward continuous improvement.

To get the best out of this book I suggest that you work with a team to try and test the ideas. The feedback from various perspectives will help you to quickly find what approaches are working well and what aren't.

Before you get your team together I recommend that you read this book at least once on your own to familiarise yourself with the approaches and the steps. By understanding the steps and the process that you are about to go through you will be better prepared when it comes to running your initial improvement sessions.

Select / invite a team of people who can reflect on the different parts of your business. By getting various points of view on this exercise you will be creating a better solution for your business. The more information (and perspectives) you have about a subject the better the decisions you can make about it. Whilst I don't want you to get into a 'management by committee' situation, doing it alone is never as good as doing it with a handful of other people.

There are a number of different approaches you can take with continuous improvement that are detailed in this book. I recommend discussing these approaches with your team to find out their feelings on the matter so that you can decide which approach(es) make most sense. Once this is agreed the next step is to then plan how you will test and use the improvement approaches that have been chosen.

Next, get the team together and try one of the approaches. Keep it light, keep it fun and keep it focussed on making your business improve. The steps of the processes are designed so that people can get fully involved with the idea generation activity. Working out the steps to implement the ideas comes later and can be avoided at the start. Evaluating the ideas generated during an improvement generation activity sometimes dampens down the session's overall effectiveness. For this reason the idea generation and the 'how to' elements are kept separate.

You may also need to make plenty of blank paper / flipcharts available so that ideas can be recorded. Encouragement of all ideas should be welcomed.

If you have a team that have issues with the business generally then it may be a good idea to vent these at the start of an improvement session. Write them down, discuss them briefly (diffusing where possible) and then agree not to discuss them again during the session. If people wander back onto their 'chosen subjects' then you can politely remind them of their previous agreement!

Once you have completed the steps provided in this book it is time to make some decisions about how you want to improve your business. It is at this point that we must take our observations and insights from doing this exercise, rationalise them, and put them into action. Our last task in this book is to make an improvement plan.

# Principles to Consider for Effective Continuous Improvement

Continuous improvement isn't difficult if you approach it in a simple and controlled manner. With this in mind let's consider some of the following principles.

## Be gentle - change is hard for most

For many people change is a hard process. Go easy on your team, be supportive and guiding and the improvements will appear. As with the example in the previous section, if you keep providing a supportive environment and the right tools then you can achieve a situation where ideas are generated and implemented by people other than yourself.

## Pareto Principle

If you are familiar with the Pareto Principle (also known as the 80/20 principle) then you will recognise that the world is skewed. Some improvements will have a large impact and cost little, some won't. If you can identify which improvement opportunities are going to give you the biggest return for your efforts then you can wisely invest your time and focus.

## Emphasise your brand

Make your business stand out by making your processes emphasise what you want to be known for. If you have spent time and money on deciding how you want your business to thought of then it makes sense that your improvement activities support this same activity. For example, it is not a good plan to want to be known for developing new technologies when your business doesn't have a good process to do just that.

## Good old QCD

Quality, Cost and Delivery - keep making these areas better and better. When you think you have gotten as far as you can it is time for a break from working on these items. After your (short) break, come back to them and see what new insights you have to improve the performance further.

## Delight the customer

If you don't have customers you don't have a business - focus on making them and their experience with you fantastic. For many businesses doing this is about taking away the obstacles that you have put in place; less obstacles often means more business.

## Persistence and Consistency

Overnight transformation is unlikely. Continuous improvement is a habit that needs to be nurtured and maintained to realise its benefits. It may take a degree of faith at the start of this work, but if you look at the improvement opportunities currently before you, you should be able to identify the benefits. You will only achieve the benefits if you persist and, if necessary, take an alternative route if you have to. This book offers you a few different approaches to consider.

## Support

Implementing the changes can take time and require overcoming difficulties; you may need to help those that struggle with doing this for themselves. What is simple to you may be incredibly difficult to someone else. Don't assume that people are, or are not, experts at improving business processes. Find the right level at which to work with others and develop their improvement abilities. It is rare to find someone who can be told, or shown, once how to use continuous improvement techniques and then master business process improvement solely on their own. Give your team the time and attention that they need.

Use this list of principles to reflect upon should you have any difficulties with your continuous improvement activities in the future. Sometimes reflecting upon these points can be all it takes to re-invigorate your existing continuous improvement approach.

# Commit to Improving

It may seem an odd thing to say 'commit to improving', but this is one of the main stumbling blocks many businesses have to overcome. Many businesses say that they are going to stick with a continuous improvement approach but rarely do. Be clear with yourself and your team (and the rest of the business) about what it means to undertake continuous improvement.

There are going to be disagreements to overcome, friction to put up with, realising that you could do it an even better way, allowing others to see what you really get up to, and more. By executing a continuous improvement process properly you are committing to stopping, thinking and acting on a regular basis. You are committing to potentially doing things differently.

More importantly you are committing to making your business the best it can be.

You may well find that you create new problems by solving old ones, but trust me - this is worth it in the long run. It doesn't take a lot of work to outpace the competition; it just takes some time and effort. Perfection can take a lot longer however, so let's focus on becoming amazing in a short period of time and then we can stroll to perfection from that point onwards.

Are you committed to making this process work?

# Method One: The Focal Points Method

This method is one of my favourites. I use it with a lot of my clients as it helps to create a simple framework that can help the business to focus on generating improvement ideas. The following pages will take you step by step through the process of using this approach.

## Step One: Split Your Business into Areas of Interest

Across the business are a number of different teams or functions, I'll refer to them as areas of interest for the time being. What are these areas of interest? They could be the departments that deal with order fulfilment within the business (purchasing, production, etc...), they could be the service teams (accounts, HR, marketing etc...), or they could be cells of customer focussed activity.

However you define your business structure make a list of these with your improvement team.

It is worth deciding at this point what the scope is for improving your business. If you are not looking at your entire business then determine how many departments / teams / cells you will need to include when creating your list.

## Step Two: Define the Factors for Improvement

The next step is to determine all of the factors that can be improved across your business. These factors could be anything that you believe could make a difference to how your business performs if made better. It might help if you think of these factors as characteristics, to describe how your business works. Below are some areas that you can consider before creating the list for your business.

### Brand

What does your business stand for? Brand is obviously much more than the logo that it bears, but what is your brand? The question that we should be asking here is - 'does the way your business work emphasise your brand?'

Simply put, if your business prides itself on fast turnarounds but its invoicing process is a total nightmare and takes forever then you have a process that detracts from the brand. Every action that is undertaken in the business needs to be consistent with the brand. This is why including your brand elements into the continuous improvement mix can be so beneficial.

**7 + 1 wastes**

If you're familiar with the lean manufacturing / lean service philosophies then you will recognise these wastes immediately. For those of you who aren't they are:

- Defects (doing things incorrectly)
- Overproduction (producing more than is required)
- Transport (moving people / material around unnecessarily)
- Waiting (delays between processes that shouldn't be there)
- Inventory (holding too much stock that may become obsolete)
- Motions (tiring people out from bad organisation of the workplace)
- Processes (a lack of optimisation in how the process runs)

The last one in our list (the '+1') is Untapped Human Potential. This is probably the most important one in the list as it means that you have minds full of ideas in your business every day and yet rarely take advantage of all of this insight and creativity that is sitting right next to you. Getting people involved with a continuous improvement process is a great way to harness this rich resource.

## QCD

As mentioned in the principles section, Quality, Cost and Delivery are tried and tested indicators of how you are performing. Improving these factors over time will help you to be recognised as a supplier of choice and could lead to increased sales due to your rock solid performance as a business to work with.

## Delighters and Satisfiers

Finally in our list of ideas is the notion of delighters and satisfiers. If you think about your own business you should be able to come up with a list of things that you would expect to be present. This could include having a tidy workplace, running short professional meetings, consistent marketing messages etc... These are satisfiers and we need to make sure that all parts of our business (or, areas of interest) conform to these standards. The delighters however are the characteristics of your business that don't have to be there, but will make the majority of your customers sit up and say 'Wow! That's amazing'. This will of course be dependent upon your area of business, but lightening fast response to queries or ultra simple ordering processes may give you this response. Over time delighters become expected and hence they become satisfiers.

Now that you have read this list - what are the characteristics that you and your team want to build and develop within your business?

Create a list of these characteristics now.

## Step Three: Create the schedule grid / date check

The next step is to create our schedule grid. We quite simply create a matrix with the areas of interest across the top of the grid and the improvement factors down the side. An example of this is shown below:

| | Sales Order Intake | Production | Invoicing |
|---|---|---|---|
| Faster | | | |
| Easier | | | |
| Friendlier | | | |

By creating this grid we now have a simple, but effective, tool for directing your continuous improvement conversations. When you have created your grid you may need to review the size of the grid. In many cases a degree of rationalisation has to take place as the current list of factors and areas of interest may be too large. Of course, you may only find this out by trying the grid out during the improvement sessions.

Print out the grid on the largest piece of paper you can and place it somewhere prominent where people can see it and be reminded that you are going to be improving the business together.

Example grids can be downloaded via the link in the Resources section and can give you a good place to start.

## Step Four: Initial review

On your improvement grid you may decide that certain areas are in need of some attention sooner rather than later. With your team review the grid for any obvious areas of concern and highlight the relevant box(es) according to the area and the type of improvement needed.

In the example, on the next page, the sales order intake process needs to be friendlier, the production process needs to be faster and the invoicing process made easier. These are highlighted by the coloured cells.

| | Sales Order Intake | Production | Invoicing |
|---|---|---|---|
| Faster | | | |
| Easier | | | |
| Friendlier | | | |

If these areas are deemed to be important areas of

improvement it is worthwhile focussing on these areas until control has been regained before moving on to the rest of the improvement combinations.

The way that this grid has been set up has been done so for two main options as to how to use it going forwards.

The first option is to choose blocks of improvement within a process, so that information can be gathered beforehand and a whole raft of ideas are created at the same time for a range of improvement factors. These blocks can be identified on the grid and dates for reviews can be added.

The second option is to use the grid to randomly select an area at the start of the improvement meeting to create a fresh and less scripted improvement discussion. If facts, figures and analysis are required then the meeting can be stopped and re-convened at a later time. The review dates would then be added once a combination had been considered.

The second option allows for more free flowing ideas and potentially shorter meetings if only one combination is chosen per session. I would recommend starting with the approach of option two if you are unsure how you would like to proceed.

## Step Five: Generate Ideas

To use this 'focal points' method you can incorporate this grid into your existing meetings, or hold a specific continuous improvement meeting.

The grid selection chosen for that session is therefore the focus of the idea generation. From the above example you may have chosen 'Invoicing : Easier' from our highlighted options. Ask the team to come up with ideas to make your invoicing process easier and let the ideas flow.

When you have completed the generation of ideas you can simply tick off that box from your grid (or put a date in it), ready to work on something else next time.

This tool is useful when asking your team to generate ideas. The focus is the key here. Not everyone is able to look at a business broadly and generate meaningful ideas. This tool is a good way to generate useful ideas and I have seen it being used to great effect by my clients. I hope that you will find it to be useful too.

# Method Two: Seasons

Method two is fundamentally an extension of the previous approach. For some businesses the grid like approach to generating ideas feels too overwhelming. The 'seasons' approach is a reduced version that can still provide enough focus to generate meaningful business improvement ideas.

The basis of this approach is to use a calendar to drive the focus in the business. Instead of leaping from one improvement area and characteristic to another, you would stay with a particular improvement characteristic for between one and three months (although you can change the timeframe as you wish). During this time you would apply it to the whole business and generate ideas accordingly.

So, to make this work you will need to choose your top level themes. This is the same as in step two in the previous method. Create a list of the different characteristics that you could apply to your business. Simple.

The next step is to create a simple time table. An example of this can be found in the resources section. If you opted for a one month time frame you could have an improvement characteristic for each month in the year.

For example:

- January: Reducing cost
- February: Shortening lead times
- March: Simplifying the customer experience
- Etc...

As with the other methods shared in this book you will need to create some form of routine to ensure that enough ideas are being generated and worked on to yield the desired benefits. Adding the idea generation activity to the end of an existing team meeting is one such way.

# Method Three: Blitz

The next method I would like to touch upon is the blitz approach. It is often called the 'Kaizen Blitz' method and fundamentally it is about focussing on one area of the business and applying improvements constantly until you experience the performance gain you were looking to achieve. On this very point, something that I have noticed time and time again, businesses often fail to see improvements through to the end. They will try something and when it doesn't work immediately it gets left and forgotten about. I will touch on this point again at the end of this book. Blitzing is a good way to stick with something until it yields benefits and therefore can, to a degree, circumvent the problem of flitting between improvements.

The first step in this method therefore is to choose a single department to improve. A process may be too large and a single operation too small. You need to choose something to work on that will provide enough challenge for a small team improving the area / process / department but not be too overwhelming. Between you and your team you will need to define a suitable scope. Going back to the selection of your team, it is still useful to have different viewpoints when blitzing, but perhaps have a higher proportion of people from the working area for this approach. If practicable, all of the people involved in the working area / process should be involved to some degree. You will need to determine this based on availability of the team members.

All of the improvement characteristics I discussed in the first method can then be used to generate improvements in the selected area. Any concerns or issues that are raised during the process need to be captured also.

The proposed schedule of activity in a blitz is as follows.

In the first step of the blitz it's all about collecting facts and issues, including Key Performance Indicator (KPI) information.

The second step is generating ideas and improvement suggestions. Use a variation of the focal points approach here if ideas are not coming quickly enough.

The third step is to prioritise the quick wins and get some action going.

The fourth step is to plan out the remaining improvements; short, medium and long term.

The fifth step is to monitor the KPIs for changes whilst managing the activity to gauge progress.

The sixth step is to crystallise the improvements into the business, so that the change becomes 'business as usual'.

The seventh step is to exit the area and hand over the improvement plans (often medium and long term) to the person responsible for the ongoing management of the area.

Although I will touch on the selection and management of improvement plans later on I would just like to mention getting some progress going. The whole idea of a blitz is that resource, time and effort is concentrated into one area of the business at a time. When all of the ideas are coming in it can be overwhelming to deal with all of the things to consider. On this basis I recommend engaging in some 'sprints' to knock off a number of the tasks. The rationale I use for choosing sprint items is that they have to be easy, have some kind of tangible benefit and that there is a motivation present in the team to see the improvement put in place. The sprint itself is simply a focussed period of time where action can take place. Protect the time of others if you need them to do something as part of this, but get some progress going. The purpose of a sprint is to get some momentum going with regard to the overall improvement piece.

If your team aren't used to making changes then a sprint can help to get people into the right frame of mind. Get people used to testing ideas and making decisions for themselves. Make sure that the improvements being selected for sprints are relatively easy and won't cause a significant impact if they go wrong. Building confidence, momentum and skills in your teams should be the major benefit of conducting this form of activity. Help everyone to see that benefits are just round the corner and any victories as part of the sprints should be shared and praised whenever possible.

I mentioned KPIs above. Many businesses undertake improvement activities and don't use this type of information to work out where they are and where they have gone to. Arguably KPIs are one of the best ways to work out if you have made a difference or not. At the end of the day, if all you have to show is a lot of work it might be hard to convince anyone of the benefits. On the other hand if you have a lot of results to demonstrate then you will have something worth showing people. In some cases developing project specific KPIs might be appropriate. These KPIs might then be discarded once the project has been a success as hopefully by then the other business KPIs will be picking up the benefits / change in performance.

The closeout of improvements is one of the most important parts of the business improvement activity. Too many times have I witnessed an improvement taking place only to watch it get lost in the fog of day to day working. There are many ways to build in new working practices into the business:

- Standard Operating Procedures (SOPs) are a common way to capture the new processes and share the information with colleagues and (especially) new starters.
- Training sessions are useful to ensure that the ideas are communicated and practiced where possible.
- Memos can be helpful when you want to raise awareness of a new process.
- Standard meetings can be used to good effect as triggers for instigating the correct process steps.
- Checklists and timetables can also be used to help instil the right tasks and activities, when a process change deems it necessary.

There are many more ways, and you just need to find the right style that fits you and your business to help develop the right habits and behaviours.

Like all continuous improvement activities the gains need to be sustainable. If you are descending upon a department to conduct a blitz type activity then working closely with the person who heads the department is a good way to proceed. At the end of the day they need to manage the rest of the improvements and conduct business as per the new processes. Doing it to them is less effective than doing it with them.
Blitzing sessions can be built into a calendar in a similar fashion to the last method, "Seasons". A programme of ongoing blitzing can be good for a business, but it may be that a combination of the approaches in this book are more suitable for your business than any one single approach.

# Method Four: Reverse Brainstorm

The reverse brainstorm is one of the easiest tools to use and never fails to put some ideas on the table. The reason that reverse brainstorming works so well is that it is easy to tear something down rather than building it up. When you choose a process to improve you simply rip it apart - what would a truly awful version be like? What doesn't work with what we already have? How could it be even worse?

Think up some negative questions like these and try them out - be ruthless! Once you have a list go back through the list and reverse the statements into something that is truly positive. Flip the worst case answers and make them the best case for each statement.

From this new list of ideas which one(s) could work well and be worth taking forward?

For example, we could use the issue of making our marketing cycle work more effectively, so...

**Negative statement**: Marketing is really expensive

**Positive statement**: Marketing is low cost

**New idea**: Analyse all marketing approaches and calculate the cost per lead to increase future impact

Another example:

**Negative statement**: It takes all day to write advertising copy

**Positive statement**: Writing copy takes seconds

**New idea**: Harvest good copy from past documents and create a more formulaic approach that receives a final 'fine tune' so that it doesn't look 'cut and pasted'

That's it. Like all good methods it is both simple and effective.

# Method Five: Role Models

The use of role models has been around for a long time. If you look at the magazines that populate many of the shelves in newsagents and shops you will see 'role models' covering the front covers. Whether these are good role models is another discussion but, just as many people look up to celebrities for their inspiration, your business could look to another business for the same reason.

To use the role models approach to generating improvement ideas you need to do a few things.

Firstly, you need to get clear as to what part of your business you are trying to improve. For this approach to work you need to quite specific about what is in scope.

Secondly, you need to identify a role model business to draw ideas from. It doesn't matter what industry or sector they come from as long as they are world class at whatever it is that you want to improve.

Thirdly, you need to ask yourself questions around how they do what they are famous for.

E.g.

"How does X* manage their changeovers?"

"What does X do with staff training?"

"When does X decide their projects are complete?"

"How does X handle their purchasing activities?"

* where X needs to be replaced by your role model's name.

From going through this process you can generate a wide range of improvement ideas. This method works best when you are using a business outside of your industry sector. Comparing your business with your competitors may not give you enough of a difference in viewpoints to draw meaningful conclusions.

# Define the Improvement's Tasks

Now that you have read all of my proposed methods to stimulate the identification of improvement ideas I thought it would be worthwhile to look at another common problem. Once businesses have generated opportunities to improve their business a question that often comes up is 'what do you do next in order to make that into a project, and what are the steps?"

If this is a question you find yourself asking, I recommend you try the 'B to A' planning method I will discuss in this section. B to A is a simple method to work from the end of an improvement project (when the goal is achieved) and work backwards to where you are today. Although many people are good at identifying the initial steps in an improvement plan it is often the final steps that people struggle with and B to A can be effective if this is the same for you.

To use the B to A approach start with your completed goal and ask yourself:

"What was the last thing I did before I got here?"

Write down your answer.

Repeat the question "what was the last thing I did before I got here?"

Write down your answer.

Keep on repeating this process until you get back to where you are today.

It can take a bit of practice to get the hang of doing this, but can help you to quickly map out the necessary steps to complete an improvement plan. Some of my clients also like to consider what they know about 'A to B' as well, to test the logic / sequence of the early steps. I also find that if you review the list once it has been completed you will often elect to re-arrange the items in the list to further improve the effectiveness of the plan.

Using this method I hope that you will be able to fill the gaps created by generating improvement ideas, leaving you with workable project plans.

I always think an example helps, so below is a B to A sequence for 'improving stock replenishment in an MRP system':
- Monitor (ongoing) requests to purchase materials.
- Develop monitoring report for purchased materials.
- Deliver training to team.
- Write SOPs and training materials.

- Define new process.
- Conclude testing phase.
- Test ideas and options in MRP.
- Generate options to test in MRP and evaluate.
- Pin point MRP modules to test.
- Review information to find problem areas.
- Crunch data to provide meaningful information.
- Gather data related to problem.
- Specify data required to understand problem.
- Scope which materials are under review.

This list may make more sense if you start at the bottom and work back up the list. Hopefully you can see the logic, even if you don't use MRP systems, and how to apply this to your own situation.

# Managing the Improvements

Now that you and your team have a preferred approach to generating improvement ideas the challenge is to manage the ongoing process. As I said at the start of this book, one of the problems with continuous improvement is the fact that it often isn't continuous. This section looks at ways to overcome this.

## Capturing Improvement Ideas

Having a method to generate improvements (moving you from OK to excellent, for example) is one thing. Knowing how you will capture or collect these improvement ideas is another.

My favourite approach is to make it routine. If you have weekly meetings then you can attach a continuous improvement review to the agenda if time permits. This can then allow you to generate new ideas, discuss existing ideas and close off completed projects.

You also need to be able to deal with the ad-hoc improvement suggestions that find their way into discussions and meetings. Capturing these opportunities into a log of some sort will help you keep hold of these ideas and help you prioritise them in the future.

Events also need to be considered. If you use the blitz option then you need to be prepared to grab all of the opportunities that come out of it.

Wherever the ideas come from, having some form of simple spreadsheet, or list, to capture the ideas is paramount. There is an example later in this section.

## Prioritisation

As you have limited time available to you during your working week to undertake extra projects, some form of prioritisation will need to take place. The simplest way of doing this is to score each improvement for the factors of ease, impact and cost. If you multiply the scores together you will get a total, and the totals can then be ranked from the largest value to the smallest.

For example:

Ease: 1 = Impossible / 10 = easy

Impact: 1 = no noticeable change / 10 = massive ROI and performance gains

Cost: 1 = prohibitively expensive / 10 = free

I should add here that motivation may also want to be considered. There may be projects that are technically difficult, giving good impacts and are low cost. The difficulty may score them lower, but this challenge may be of interest to the people on your team. If there is motivation present then it is certainly worth harnessing and putting to good use.

Some scores may be so high that you just want to get on and do them. If you have some kind of sign off process for changes then it may be worth reviewing the thresholds to determine which projects can be implemented immediately and which ones need to wait for authorisation. This streaming approach may help smaller projects get off the ground quicker. Larger projects (those with costs involved) may need to have a business case put forward and for obvious reasons slow down progress.

## Routine Improvement Meeting

If you have been reading this book and thought to yourself that having a short formal improvement meeting is a good idea then I would agree. With the right agenda and right preparation you can get a lot done in fifteen minutes. Once you have your people organised, the next steps are to choose a frequency for the meetings and create a meaningful agenda.

A good agenda is simple, effective and short. This allows people to keep focussed on the meeting at hand, before leaving to get on with their other day-to-day priorities. Before we look at an example agenda you need to consider how often you are going to meet to generate ideas and track progress. This frequency will depend on the situation that you are facing. If you are under significant pressure and need to implement some changes rapidly then daily may be appropriate, but if things are going well and you are fine tuning existing established processes then weekly or fortnightly may be more suitable.

One word of warning with this is that this process needs to be done routinely. If you choose a weekly slot, for example, then you need to make sure that it happens at the same time every week without fail. Make sure that you have holiday cover and that people are reprimanded if they don't attend. This improvement meeting will become a disciplined part of the work place if done correctly. Improvement sessions are mostly fun, but are a serious undertaking at the same time.

**Example Agenda**

- Choose a focus to work on. (This could be the next box from the matrix, changing the 'season' to focus on or a specific process.)
- Generate ideas (use reverse brainstorm / role models if required).
- Add new ideas to the list and score.
- Prioritise and select ideas to take forward.
- List necessary actions / responsibilities to action plan.
- Review the progress made since last session / update plan.
- Discuss blitz areas for consideration / plan next blitz.
- Close.

## Track Improvements

One of the important features of continuous improvement is the ability to track the improvement ideas, to manage them through implementation and then to check that the improvement has taken effect and has been firmly established within the business as the current way of working.

You will most likely recognise this as the Plan Do Check Act method, commonly abbreviated to PDCA. I include this for two main reasons. Firstly, it is simple, effective and works. Secondly, I find many people too quickly dismiss an improvement idea because it doesn't work the first time around. If you have studied PDCA you will be acutely aware that half of the cycle is to Check and then Act. Knowing how close an improvement idea / trial came to delivering its results and what you need to do in order to modify the result is essential in continuous improvement.

Below is an example of how this approach can be used to record improvements. Modify it to suit your needs and use it with your improvement meetings. An example can be downloaded from the resources section.

The last column (furthest right) is probably the most critical. Once you have proven your idea and it is working you will need to work out how to properly close out the action. This may be updating maintenance records (or creating them in the first place!), writing a new instruction for the business / standard operating procedure, updating training plans etc...

The key is that you do something formal with the new information so that your business does not lose this improved way of working over time (just because people forget or leave).

Improvement Project Tracking Log

| Issue | Improvement Idea | Tasks | Responsible | Due Date | Checked Date | Close Out Method |
|---|---|---|---|---|---|---|
| | | | | | | |

You may have also noticed the first column, 'issue'. In some cases you won't have spotted the improvement idea, but you will have spotted the issue or concern you have around a process. This column is designed to let you capture other issues that people are having with your business' processes, without the need for stating an improvement idea. This allows for team work to be built into your continuous improvement approach as it may be that someone from another team has the solution to someone else's problem.

Scheduling the improvement projects should also be considered when defining due dates. For any business there will only be so many projects that can be undertaken at any one time. Also, having too many changes taking place at any one time could be counterproductive, so please schedule with care.

## Communication

Informing your teams, and wider staff, about the progress of the continuous improvement projects is vital to the longevity and buy in for your ongoing efforts. As much as people can appear strong and independent, they usually need to know that their ideas are valued and are being considered in a proper way.

To keep your team in the picture as to where their ideas are the improvement log can be very useful if this is made publicly available. I discussed earlier the need for prioritisation and if this is visible and ranked (work in progress, followed by queued in order of priority) then it can let people know where their ideas are.

This same list can also help your team to understand what is coming their way in terms of changes.

Having someone centrally responsible for the improvements list / schedule can make it easier to communicate what is happening next. This information can then be fed to the rest of the business via routine team meetings or by an update circulated physically (on notice boards for example) or electronically. A combination of team meetings and written updates works well. This approach also allows you to take the opportunity of letting the teams know why and how the change is happening. Having a good reason behind an improvement project can make a big difference. Let's not forget face to face conversation either. If time permits, speaking to people (that you probably pass anyway) can be really effective and should not be forgotten about in light of email / notice board based communication already being in place.

Keeping your staff up to date with the improvement plans helps keep the entire continuous improvement efforts moving along nicely.

## Improvement Idea Life Span

Before I finish this section of the book I want to touch upon the priority system once more. There is a good chance that suggestions that get made never make it into the actual programme of change. Some of the ideas may be too expensive or too difficult to implement. Rather than clog up the list / spreadsheet that you use to list your opportunities you may choose to give your improvement ideas a life span. Somewhere between six months and a year is appropriate for most businesses.

For those opportunities that are too prohibitive to undertake I suggest that you archive them. Don't lose the idea altogether as you never know when the situation may change and the idea could be just right.

For the other group of opportunities I feel that you have two options to consider. If the idea is fundamentally good, but just didn't have a high enough score to make it into the schedule of activity then the two options become; do it now anyway or archive it. Taking action on ideas in this manner, as long as they don't cost a great deal to implement, can be good for morale and is therefore worth considering, helping maintain the continuous improvement momentum.

# Maintain Your Continuous Improvement System

As time moves on it becomes necessary, as it does for any system, to review how the system is working.

How you conduct your improvement idea generating sessions should be reviewed as should the nature in which you capture and retain the ideas from these sessions. The prioritisation method you use and your ability to select the right improvements should be reviewed to ensure that the outcome is still the best it can be.

If you are using the 'focal points' method then the elements of the grid that are being used may want to be refreshed. You may have already been through several iterations of your grid and it may be time to change the focus slightly.

The same can be said of any of the other methods proposed in this book; different seasons, different role models, different blitz methods.

In its truest sense, this is continuous improvement. It is usual to improve the method of managing the process as you will most likely have a range of new insights and perspectives that come from running the system for a while.

Another consideration is that of the capability and capacity of your team. The early projects may have to be a little easier for your team to undertake due to the newness of the situation. As projects get completed it is usual for people's confidence to grow as their abilities develop. The rate of progress may increase and their effective capacity for implementing change may grow. When you are scheduling your improvement projects it is worth bearing this in mind.

The biggest question to ask, however, when reviewing how your system is working is this one.

"Does this approach deliver tangible results?"

I hope that the answer is yes. If it is not then please review the activities that you have undertaken and try to look for the cause and (lack of?) effect relationship. Please don't keep running a system that isn't working, make the necessary changes so that tangible benefits can be realised. If the ideas are good and the execution is good, as is the handover and sustainability then you should be able to reap the rewards. If this is not the case then review each of the elements (quality of ideas, evaluation, implementation, close out / handover and making it routine / sustainable) to find opportunities to improve.

# Developing Your Approach

It is now time for you to define how you want to approach your continuous improvement system for your own business.

There are a number of things you may consider:

- Choose how you want to generate ideas. Do you like the idea of a formal weekly meeting, capturing ad-hoc ideas, or blitzing? Do you like a combination of all the methods put forward?

- Choose how you want to work with your team. How much autonomy do you want them to have? How much support will they need at the start? Are there guidelines you want to put in place so your team are clear when they need to get your approval and when it is OK to test without your input?

- How do you want to capture the ideas and prioritise them? Are there ideas in this book that will suit your business, or do you have something already that you can use?

- Figure out how much time you have to implement change per week. After the 'day job' how much time is left over (if any!)? Planning to use more than half of this time is possibly unrealistic, circumstances may still work against you.

- Choose a coordinator for your improvements. Who will oversee the planning and scheduling of the improvement activities? Your answers to the previous point will inform the scheduling activity.

- Measure the results of each improvement. Can you do this via your existing KPIs? Will you need to create some forms of temporary measurement? How will you measure success?

I hope that this book has given you some ideas on how to develop your own continuous improvement system. Developing your own style that suits both you and your business will make the system naturally more sustainable than just using it 'off the shelf'.

# Troubleshooting

Even with a well thought out continuous improvement approach you may still run into problems getting it off the ground. The following three points are all aimed at getting your improvement activities up and running in the way that they were intended to.

## If your team doesn't have time to work on the projects

This is one of the most common objections. Two good methods for pushing past this are to block out the first half an hour at the start of the working day for working on improvement activity (and no more) until the benefits start appearing, or to pick the improvement that takes the least amount of time to work on. By seeing the improvements materialise people will be more willing to do more, and hopefully as they become both more efficient and more effective they will have more time in their day as a result.

Getting momentum early on in the projects is vital to build enough interest and support so that it can carry on under its own steam.

## If good ideas are thrown out too early

This where the plan, do, check and act (PDCA) tool comes in again. Before your team throw away an improvement idea because it isn't working, it is worth reviewing how close you came to achieving the result and trying to work out if you can repeat the approach in a slightly different manner. Often a small tweak to an approach can make a big difference. Education of the people involved with making the idea work coupled with persistence and a willingness to listen to feedback is a potent mix for getting ideas to work.

Also, having someone as part of your team 'authorise' ideas being archived (or whatever you would call this) can help to ensure that ideas are scrutinised to some degree to make sure that there is really no merit with progressing with the idea at this point in time.

## If your team aren't making progress

If this is the case then make the activity required, or the time to be spent, or the objectives, smaller. Keep making them smaller until your team think nothing of the requirements. Once started support them to increase the size of the task / objective and let the activity grow with their confidence.

This is known, more popularly, as Kaizen. The 'fight or flight' response often manifests itself in the workplace as procrastination. Combating procrastination with tiny steps is a great method and can quickly generate results. It may look like tiny steps could take forever to complete a project, but having faith in people to gain confidence and momentum can change this picture entirely. It does take additional support however, but if the benefits are worth it then so is the support. This Kaizen approach is the instigator behind the 'focal points' method I discussed earlier on in this book.

These are just three quick ideas for you to consider, the ones I see on a regular basis that work. I hope they help you to make progress too.

# Supporting Approaches

In addition to the methods shared in this book there are a few more I would like to briefly share before we end our journey together.

## CCC

The first one, 'CCC', stands for Concern, Cause, Countermeasure.

When you are trying to generate improvements and all you receive is problems, concerns and issues then this tool is great for converting them into meaningful improvements.

When the problems are being mentioned all you need to do is list them. Using a sheet that is split into three columns is perfect. In the left hand column capture all of the issues that are being shared. Do not try to solve them as they are being listed, just capture them.

Next, find the cause of the problem. Dig around the subject until you find out what is going on. Use the next technique of '5 Why' if you need to. Keep looking into the problem until you find the root cause of the issue.

Finally, define the countermeasure (or improvement project

tasks) that will help you conquer the issues raised.

## 5 Why

This is an approach to get to the root cause of problems. By asking 'why' questions you can get past symptoms and find what is really behind a problem. You may have used this approach already in your normal business activities as it is a great tool in its own right. For businesses that are new to this approach I find that the most common cause of not using it is a lack of engagement when asking the questions.

The quickest way to lose the engagement is just to ask 'why?' The best way to engage with your subject is to consider the answer and then ask a more specific 'why?' question. For example:

- Why does that happen on a Tuesday morning?
- Why can this exist if we have already done the process in the right sequence?
- Why haven't we considered implementing this idea before?

It can take a bit of practice to become proficient at asking meaningful why questions, but being able to focus people's minds and dig below the surface of a problem is a valuable skill. The power in this approach is to keep on digging until you find something you can resolve, something that is fundamental (and in your control to resolve) and will also cure a number of other problems you have in your business.

I should also point out that if you get to a point in your enquiry where you need to go away and get some factual information then please do. Continuing with your 'why?' questions without having proper information may lead you down the wrong path.

Keep going until you get an 'aha' moment. Don't try and solve a symptom, solve a root cause.

## Facts and Pareto (or, 80 / 20)

Often decisions are made based on limited observations or, worse, are a knee jerk reaction to pressure being felt to make a change. If this resonates with you then try to gather more information to make an enlightened decision. When you do gather information there is usually a pattern that forms - where one or two factors outweigh the rest. This is known as the Pareto principle which states that 80% of the effects are caused by 20% of the causes.

I touched upon this earlier in the book and it is a realisation that the world is wonky, there is not usually a neat, evenly distributed, pattern to results. The numbers don't always come out so neatly as 80 / 20, but in most cases a wonky result is returned. This means that you can single out the few issues that are causing you a real problem and 'ignore' the rest until you have more time and resources to resolve them. If you solve a handful of big problems (and the causes may not be big at all to remedy) then you have you used your time and energy more efficiently.

# Final Thoughts

Continuous improvement can be a simple process to follow if you follow the principles and methods laid out in this book. Continuous improvement doesn't have to be left to chance. It can be done in a more formulaic way as presented in this book. It doesn't stifle the creativity of the business by doing it in this way - it helps to release creativity through focus on issues that need to be made better.

Continuous improvement doesn't have to take a lot of time either. Even five minutes per week on coming up with ideas can generate more ideas than can be implemented in a working week. Using the matrix can generate almost instant ideas on how to improve so, if anything, perhaps short sessions should be encouraged. This can work really well if you have smaller teams.

Continuous improvement can be fun. A laugh and a joke shared during one of your routine meetings can be very useful and if the sessions are fun then people will be willing to take part, and when they're willing ideas will flow. Use the 'routine meetings' and 'formal agenda' to (ironically) let a bit more fun into the workplace.

I think it is important to come up with your own approach to continuous improvement, to find a style that fits your way of working. I hope that you have found some thoughts, methods and ideas in this book that can help you to do just this.

Continuous improvement can make a huge difference in the workplace. It's not hard to do, can cost very little, can yield huge performance and profit benefits, can help develop your staff...

...so what's stopping you from getting started?

# Links and Resources

## Continuous Improvement Resources

To download the quick start templates and the other resources described in this book please visit:

**http://www.ci.smartspeed.co.uk**

## Smartspeed Blog

For more ideas on how to improve your business and to find out how to apply some of the more common business improvement ideas in novel ways please visit our blog:

**http://www.systemsandprocesses.co.uk/blog**

## Free On Time Delivery Report

If you want some ideas about how to improve the on time delivery performance of your business, then please download our free report. You will need to register your email address on our website, the link is:

**http://www.systemsandprocesses.co.uk**

## LinkedIn OTIF Forum

If you would like to join us online to discuss practical ideas about improving on time delivery performance then please visit our LinkedIn group:

**http://www.linkedin.com/groups/On-Time-Delivery-Improvement-4419220/about**

# About Giles Johnston

Giles is a Chartered Engineer with a background in Operations Management who spends most of his time working on capacity planning and 'on time delivery' improvement projects.

He has worked in a variety of different roles within manufacturing prior to working as a consultant for a prestigious university.

In 2005 Giles decided to forge his own path and created Smartspeed, which has been helping businesses to improve their delivery performance, along with their profits, ever since.

Giles can be contacted by:

Email - **gilesjohnston@smartspeed.co.uk**

Website - **www.smartspeed.co.uk**

Printed in Great
Britain
by Amazon

32063963R00054